Red Cup Philosophy

The Unconventional Lessons of Life

Dominique J. Lee

© 2020, 2021 *Dominique J. Lee. All rights reserved.*

No part of this book may be reproduced, stored in a retrieval system, or transmitted by any means without the written permission of the author.

2nd Edition published by 8th Wonder on 7/24/2021. Originally Published by AuthorHouse 07/23/2020.

ISBN: 978-1-7375690-0-8

ISBN: 978-1-7375690-1-5

ISBN: 978-1-7283-6736-1 (sc)

ISBN: 978-1-7283-6735-4 (e)

Print information available on the last page.

Any people depicted in stock imagery provided by Getty Images are models, and such images are being used for illustrative purposes only. Certain stock imagery © Getty Images.

This book is printed on acid-free paper.

Because of the dynamic nature of the Internet, any web addresses or links contained in this book may have changed since publication and may no longer be valid. The views expressed in this work are solely those of the author and do not necessarily reflect the views of the publisher, and the publisher hereby disclaims any responsibility for them.

Scripture quotations marked NLT are taken from the Holy Bible, New Living Translation, copyright © 1996, 2004, 2007. Used by permission of Tyndale House Publishers, Inc. Carol Stream, Illinois 60188. All rights reserved. Website

Scripture quotations marked KJV are from the Holy Bible, King James Version (Authorized Version). First published in 1611. Quoted from the KJV Classic Reference Bible, Copyright © 1983 by The Zondervan Corporation.

Scripture quotations marked NKJV are taken from the New King James Version. Copyright © 1982 by Thomas Nelson, Inc. Used by permission. All rights reserved.

To the individuals who have poured into my life, this book is respectfully dedicated.

Table of Contents

THE PRE-GAME I

GOOD MORNING 1

EVERYBODY WASN'T RAISED BY CHELL 7

NEWTON'S THREE LAWS OF MOTION 11

EVERY TUB MUST SIT ON ITS OWN BOTTOM 17

LEVEL UP 21

DIE EMPTY 25

I'VE BEEN TO THE MOUNTAINTOP 29

SUCCESS IS IN THE EYE OF THE BEHOLDER 33

BECAUSE I SAID SO 37

ACCURACY OVER SPEED 41

DON'T YUCK MY YUM 45

GO, YOU'LL BE FINE 49

8 TRACKS, CDS, MP3S 55

DO IT ANYHOW 59

YOU TAKE CARE NOW 63

THE PRICE OF GLORY IS HIGH 67

EATING IS A HARD HABIT TO BREAK 71

I GOT YOU	75
THE WAITING ROOM	79
I AM	83
BEING WILLING AND ABLE	87
CAN YOU STAND THE RAIN?	91
NO WORRIES STEP CLAP	97
WHO YO' FOLKS?	101
TRUST YOUR GIFT	105
ONLY YOU CAN PREVENT FOREST FIRES	109
IF YOU SEE SOMETHING, SAY SOMETHING	113
WE GOT FOOD AT THE HOUSE	117
THE CUP AND THE SAUCER	121
IF YOU CAN "HUH" ME, YOU CAN HEAR ME	125
CALL A SPADE A SPADE	129
THE RIDE HOME	135

The Pre-Game

What is the Red Cup Philosophy?

Hey Family! If you grew up anything like me, then as a child you've attended a backyard party or two. You know, that kind of weekend social gathering where friends and family would come together; with no agenda other than to just enjoy each other's company. The ones where us kids would often be found running around outside or playing among ourselves in the den, while the adults were all gathered in similar fashion in another part of the house.

During these functions, the grown-ups may enjoy a few meatballs, some Rotel dip, maybe even a chicken wing or two, all while indulging in some kind of adult beverage. No matter what, participating in a conversation that seemed to never end was always on the menu. Laughter, crying, clapping, loud talking and even random outbursts of profanity could be heard throughout the house. Eavesdropping on grown folks' conversations, I would hear things like, "The good book talks about people like you...", "Biggie Smalls put it best, 'Mo Money Mo Problems'", "You ain't shit!", or my all-time favorite, "You know Momma always said...", followed by a colloquialism that seemed to never make sense and yet somehow always brought clarity.

Whatever the topic, everyone had something to offer; an opinion, advice, a quote or even a joke to lighten the mood.

This is what I call a "Pouring Session". Essentially it's a time and space where people, without filter, share their life experiences, lessons and "ah-ha!" moments. It's in these moments that we as humans take off the mask of formalities and start "being real" to unconsciously yet undoubtedly "pour" into the lives of others for their betterment.

Any who, back to the party. Just like their diverse and continuous conversations, the grown-ups would often move from one space to another. By the end of the party the back porch, living room and kitchen all contained evidence that the adults had been there. The number one indicator: red cups.

No matter how late it ended, the adults always left these gatherings full, and not just because of the food and liquor (lol). They were full of **hope**. They were full of **joy**. They were full of a **peace** that comes with knowing that someone else had experienced similar situations and came out of it better on the other side. It was a sense of community. A feeling of familiarity.

This is Red Cup Philosophy. A concoction of scriptures, jokes, and off-the-wall quotes that forced me to think more deeply, see myself more clearly and live more abundantly. These real-life experiences and the lessons that came with them may be unconventional and hard to swallow; however, the revelations have brought me comfort, clarity, and confidence. And just like those adults, it's only right that I share these little shots of wisDOM with you.

So welcome to the party. The first round is on me!

1 Good Morning

Have you ever picked up a habit and didn't know where it came from? Chile... I know I have. For example, a while back my best friend started saying, "Good Morning" at the beginning of our conversations. Just out the blue – didn't matter what time of day we spoke; when she greeted me, it was with a "good morning." At some point, I picked up her "good morning" habit and adopted it as my own. That's about the time when she stopped saying it altogether (lol). Go figure.

I did my best to shake it but, like many other habits we collect over time, it just kept coming up. It was so embarrassing. I couldn't control it. Eventually I just gave up and began to embrace this little quirk I'd acquired. After a while I even began putting my own spin on it, emphasizing certain syllables and allowing the inflections in my voice to represent how I was feeling. It became a part of me, so much so that my friends and coworkers even started saying it back. They expected it and if I didn't say it, they knew something was wrong.

At some point I thought - there has to be something deeper to this. How did a habit I picked up from my best friend become my tagline? And more importantly, why did it stick with me of all people? Now personally, I believe that conversations with myself double as conversations with God. So when I ask questions that I can't figure out the answer to, I resolve that He will give me the answer when I need to know it.

One day while praying and meditating, I was reminded of the Mary Mary song "In the Morning." In the chorus, Erica and Tina Campbell sing:

"In the morning, you'll be alright

In the morning, the sun's gonna shine

In the morning, no clouds in the sky

When it's dark in your life just wait for the daylight"

That's when it hit me. Morning represents the beginning of something new. A refresh. A place to begin again. And with every new morning comes a renewal of His grace and mercy. Now, I know me. I know my thoughts and my mouth and I sometimes use up my daily allotment of grace and mercy before I get to work. Growing up I always read: *"... weeping may endure for a night, but joy comes in the morning." - Psalms 30:5 NKJV* and for me, I need to constantly stay in a "morning" state of mind to make it joyfully through the day.

Being my inquisitive self, my next thought was, "Why do I say it to others as opposed to just knowing it and meditating on it internally?" For that answer, I was reminded of Romans 4:17 which pretty much tells me that through faith I have the authority to speak those things that are not as though they are.

Aight, at this point, I'm floored. Up until now, I thought saying "good morning" was a meaningless tagline. However, it was clear to me now that this perceived silly habit I picked up from my best friend, that I once considered embarrassing, was actually a two-word prayer. It was my way of speaking into existence for myself and others that **IT WAS MORNING!**

You see, night and or darkness represent trying times in our lives. It represents those days, and sometimes even months, when we feel lost, confused, uncomfortable, hurt and even alone. In these uncertain times we must remember that morning is coming.

And morning does not have to be when you see the sunrise. At 12:01a.m. it may be pitch black outside, but one thing I know for sure is that it is morning. The breaking of day signifies the breaking of your current situation. And that breaking can come at any moment.

Every day that God gives you a morning He's saying, "Never mind the mistakes you made. Who cares about when you ignored my instructions? Despite what you did, who you did it with and how long you did it; there's still something in you that I can use. You still have purpose and I still find you valuable. You are still worthy of a morning."

If you believe that just look someone in the eyes, and that someone may be your own reflection, and repeat my rendition of Psalms 30:5, "Weeping…" or as some of us say, "[We] may endure for a night, oh, but Good Morning!"

Challenge:

Always speak life into situations; for yourself and for others. Practice saying "Good Morning" to people regardless of the time of day. When they look at you funny just look back and say, "Don't mind me. I'm just speaking those things that are not as though they are."

2 Everybody Wasn't Raised by Chell

To my mother and 3B (Biological Big Brother) –

Machelle Lee and Jarrod Lee

Have you ever come across someone who just didn't get it? Like, what seems to be the most logical thing to you just flies over their head? Maybe it's a co-worker, a church member or even a cousin on your daddy side (lol).

Regardless, I think it's safe to say that we've all encountered at least one individual like that. I know my older brother Jarrod and I have on several occasions. And each time we just look at each other and say, "You know, everybody wasn't raised by Chell."

Now Chell is short for Machelle. As in Machelle Lee. As in Machelle Lee our mother. And because my brother and I were the only two growing up in the house with her, it's a fact that everybody wasn't raised by Chell and got all of the lessons that came with that experience.

One lesson she taught us was to never keep a ride waiting. If we were catching a ride with someone, then they should never have to wait on us. We should be ready and waiting on them. Chell also taught us to never put a used fork, spoon or our hands in food that's shared with others. Y'all just nasty! Out here double-dipping and shit! Use a damn napkin, a serving utensil or dip some out on your plate. Hell!

We believed that these things were common sense; boy were we wrong. As we got older, Jarrod and I realized that the way we process, evaluate and make decisions derived from the experiences we endured at the hands of Chell. The chores, the no's and the yes's, the pats on the backs and the whippings altogether shaped us both into the men we are today.

No doubt we as humans are shaped by our experiences and the lessons from the experiences of those who raised us. All of these factors help to shape the way we think, our character and how we show up in the world.

I am not saying that mentors, teachers and other people such as friends, social media personalities and cultural norms don't influence us. What I am saying is that these people and communities only build upon the foundations laid by those who have nurtured and taken care of us since the day we started breathing.

The phrase, "Everybody wasn't raised by Chell", that Jarrod and I use, represents an understanding of differences. It denotes a sense of pride in our upbringing and serves as a constant reminder to operate with a level of empathy and compassion because that's what Chell taught us. It is also a reminder to not expect ourselves from others.

Unspoken expectations, in my opinion, are the number one leading cause in the demise of relationships. And not just in a romantic sense - this applies to any type of relationship, friendship, situationship or entanglement. The realization that someone just doesn't get it can be frustrating and disappointing. Now I see why Chell taught us to use grace and compassion when interacting with others. Our understanding that experiences dictate ones level of consciousness helps us be effective in our communication and just in our expectations.

The phrase also reminds me that people, problems, pressures, and praise contribute to how folks show up in the world. In the end, it's the experiences we've had and the behaviors we've acquired that molds us into who we are. So what you weren't raised by Chell; That's alright! I'll teach you what Chell taught me and you teach me what Angela, Robert, Maxine or Dexter taught you. And together, we will grow to have a better understanding of each other.

wisDOM:

Different experiences cause us to respond differently. Stop expecting you from other people and uphold the responsibility to extend grace when you encounter people with different upbringings.

3 Newton's Three Laws of Motion

At some point in science class we all were introduced to Sir Isaac Newton. The man was bad y'all! A genius. I'm talking an inventor, author and the mathematician who developed the principles of modern physics. Hands down, his most well-known findings are now known as Newton's Three Laws of Motion.

Now, you ain't got to agree with me; however, I also see my boy Newton as a philosopher. Oh yeah, the man was deep. His three laws of motion apply to more than just physics – they also apply to life.

Check it: Newton starts his three laws with the basics. "Every object at rest or in motion will respectfully remain at rest or in motion unless acted upon by force." Simply put, nothing changes until something changes.

If all I ever did was sit on a couch, then that's all I would ever do. However, if I continuously put my dreams and aspirations in motion, then something is bound to come of it. Let me make it plain.

Apply for that dream job. Work during the day and take classes at night. Go passionately towards the things you want. Stay focused and let nothing stop you because with every step you take you get closer to your destination. And once you get to going you'll realize just how hard it is to stop.

Newton's second law states: "Force equals mass times acceleration."

Have you ever been riding a bike and the brakes went

out? I mean, I've certainly found myself riding down a hill a time or two and couldn't stop. The force at which I hit the side of the house was produced by how fat I was and how fast I was going (lol).

In life, the amount of force it takes to knock down your fears is determined by the speed of your attack times how much weight you put on it. Can I say it scientifically? The amount of work you put in, multiplied by how much momentum you gain determines the impact you'll make.

The bigger your fears are, the harder your attack has to be. Put all you have into it. Be consistent. Start slow then pick up speed and watch your fears and anxieties fall by the wayside.

Newton's third law is by far my favorite. So stay with me. I'm gonna say it like this: "For every action there is an equal and opposite reaction" - commonly called a consequence. That last part was added by me (lol).

Be it good or bad, we each have to deal with the consequences of our actions. We all play a role in what happens to us. If we sit still, there's gonna be a consequence. If we turn back, there's gonna be a consequence. If we forge ahead, there's gonna be a consequence.

The goal is to minimize the chances of unwanted consequences by taking educated risks. This is done by thinking through the realities of our actions and what the potential ramifications of our choices may be. How do we do this? I'm happy you asked. In geometry we learn that this is called a conditional statement also known as an "If-Then" statement. An "If-Then" statement is an educated guess followed by an anticipated result. Stay with me now...

Here's a few examples. If I never take that leap of faith, then I will never know if I can fly. If I continue to allow you to cripple me, then I will never know what it feels like to stand on my own two feet. If I never apply for the job, then I will never get the interview. C'mon Now!

Your actions are one of the direct causes of your consequences. Don't let what you do, or don't do, keep you stagnant. Alright. I'm done preaching... for now (lol).

I told you Newton was the man. Now that you know better you have to do better. Will you put things into motion? Will you consistently attack your goals with everything you have to gain momentum? Will you start taking educated risks to get the desired outcome? I think you should. Because once you move, other things around you will move. And before you know it, you've started a movement.

Challenge:

Start. Whatever it is, start and start today. Do the research, take calculated risks and put in the work. Then wake up tomorrow and do the same thing again. And again the next day, and the next and the day after that. You may have to slow down. You may have to speed up. No matter what, just don't stop.

4 Every Tub Must Sit On its Own Bottom

To "Granny" - the late Mattie S. Woods

I grew up in a single parent home in what I affectionately call the backwoods of Alabama. And before you get to talking, let me say this up front: my father was definitely in my life, he just wasn't in my home. So one person who helped my mother raise my older brother and me was my maternal grandmother, my Granny, Mrs. Mattie S. Woods.

Growing up in the 90s with a 30 something year old mother and middle aged grandmother resulted in two protective guardians who wouldn't let me get away with anything. Like, I was not allowed to sleep over at any of my friends' houses until my junior year of high school! Momz talkin' bout, "Nah, you not gonna stay over there. I bought a bed for you to sleep in so that's where you'll be tonight." (lol) So I'm pretty sure you can imagine what happened when I went off to college.

Despite only being about 90 minutes away from home, traveling back to visit Granny and Chell was not top priority for me. I had already done two years at home while attending Central Alabama Community College, so at 20-years-old I was ready to live my life away from home.

Don't get me wrong, I was not wildin' out. I was simply enjoying being on my own, being self-sufficient and making my own decisions. As you would imagine, neither of these ladies were pleased with my decision to be so... "self-reliant." Not because I was irresponsible, but because being so hands off was new to them. I was their "Baby Boy." Letting go of the youngest wasn't easy.

During one of my sporadic trips home, Momz and Granny were going on and on about how infrequent my visits were. After seeing how little I was paying attention to them, I heard Granny say, "You know what Chell, every tub has to sit on its own bottom." And just like that my Momz dropped it. I didn't fully understand what Granny meant until years later when my mother called to give me some news.

Brace yourself. While sitting in an airport; my phone rang. It's Momz. She had something to tell me. I stepped away from the gate to a less crowded area. Then Chell fixed her mouth to say, "I've accepted my calling into the ministry." I looked at the phone in silence.

Now wait!!! You have to understand! To remix the immortal words of Tupac, I'm a Christian but don't push me (lol). I'm a work in progress; hell, I still cuss (that means I use profanity for all of you non-Southern country talking folks). So you can imagine my reaction.

I low-key think she told me while I was in public so that I couldn't react like I wanted to. Hell, even my initial thoughts were, "God, you must be a comedian today. Do you know who her child is? 'Cause it's me. I mean... you know me! And I know you look down at me and just shake your head sometimes. And you want me to be the son of a minister? Oh you got jokes today!"

She followed up my brief moment of silence with a simple, "It's just something I have to do." That's when it hit me. I understood what Granny meant when she said, "every tub must sit on its own bottom."

Choosing to step away from my old stomping grounds to fully immerse myself in a different world was what I needed to do for me, despite what the people who raised me wanted. The same was happening here with my Momz. Chell had to do what was best for her despite how I felt about her new path.

Now I'm saying the same thing to you. At some point you can no longer blame others for what you did or did not do. You have to assume responsibility for your own actions. You have to live your own life and you have to let others live theirs. Just like me and my momma, you can't concern yourself with anyone else's bottom. We each have our own we have to sit on.

wisDOM:

You gotta do what's best for you because in the end, only you are responsible for what you did and did not do.

5 Level Up

To my best friend - Ashley Oliver

It's often said that we are a reflection of the four people we talk to the most. And I couldn't agree more. My best friend Ashley and I talk just about every day. Although different, we are very much alike.

Ashley is a financially conscience, shy Southern soul who doesn't like attention. She knows when to be gentle and forgiving and she knows when to be stern and unwavering. Ashley is both negro spirituals, "Amazing Grace" and "Wipe Me Down" at the same damn time. (lol)

When I made the decision to move to New York City for grad school at New York University, Ashley and another friend offered to throw me a going away party. Of course I was on board, because who would turn down a party? However, one thing was not up for debate: Ashley had to wear makeup and weave during my party. Yes, I said makeup and weave.

Up until this point Ashley had never worn weave a day in her life and was only into makeup for special occasions. Well, this definitely qualified as a special occasion. After going back and forth on hair styles and just how much makeup she had to wear, we came to a compromise. Ashley agreed to do a natural lite look on her face and wear clip-in extensions. I won!

Ashley kept her word and wore both the makeup and extensions to my party. All night I peeped her swinging her hair and taking photos. I could tell she was feeling herself. The makeup and hair just boosted her confidence and enhanced the beauty she already possessed.

After my move, we stayed in touch via FaceTime. I noticed that Ashley was wearing makeup more often. I'd see photos of her on the 'Gram, face beat, hair blowing in the wind, just living her best life. Then, one day my phone rings. It's Ashley. I pick up and the first thing I hear is, "Dominique, I ain't shit!"

You see, this is how Ashley and I start conversations when we realize our own faults and just need to let someone else know that we know what we know.

"So what did you do now?" I replied with a chuckle. Ashley then begins to tell me that she can't stop buying makeup and hair. This girl was buying pallets of makeup just because she wanted one color out of the set. She was also buying multiple bundles, sending them to wig makers to make custom wigs for her, and still making clip-ins herself. The girl even added a makeup and hair line item in her monthly budget! I knew she had fallen in love with the beauty industry from simply observing her over the last several months; however, I didn't realize just how deep into it she was.

I was concerned, but I could also tell that this was something that made her happy. So instead of urging her to stop, I challenged her to keep doing her own makeup while looking for opportunities to express her new found love for beauty outside of her home. Truth be told, she had already been thinking the same thing. I just said out loud what she had already been saying to herself.

Fast forward a few years, Ashley now owns and operates *Beauty by Ash Styles* – a wig and makeup service company. I couldn't be more proud of her. She allowed herself to be challenged and embraced the opportunity which eventually led to a new business venture.

That's what real friends do. We make sure that each other is PROgressing and not REgressing. The only way we can do that is if we continue to push each other out of our comfort zones, hold one another accountable and force each other to level up.

Challenge:

Surround yourself around folks who make you level up. And at the same time, I challenge you to be that person for someone else.

6 Die Empty

After graduating from Alabama State University, I developed a fear of not living long enough to do all of the things I wanted to do. Simple things like take a trip to Los Angeles, California, start my own company and record a song were all goals that I feared I would never see. Some years later I heard a story about someone else's experience with that same fear and God started to embellish and personalize that thang for me. Here's what He told me through my Holy Ghost Imagination:

After I died, I would get to Heaven. Upon arrival, the angels would show me to my mansion. I'd open the door and find Jesus standing arms wide open. He'd give me the warmest hug and then say, "Welcome home my good and faithful servant."

He'd start showing me around the place with all of its many rooms, light filled spaces and floor to ceiling windows. And then we'd come to this one closet. He'd open the door and say, "In this closet are all the opportunities, experiences and joys I promised you while on earth." I'd ask, "Why are they here? Why didn't I get to enjoy them down there?" and He'd reply, "You could have, but you didn't trust me."

"You didn't trust that I was Jehovah Jireh and that I'd make a way out of no way; every time. You didn't trust that if you made one step, I'd make two. You didn't trust me when I said, 'Long as you got me you won't need nobody. If you want it, I got it. Go get it, I'll buy it. Tell them other broke jokers be quiet'." Thank you TI (lol). "Instead, you looked at your circumstances and people on social media and convinced yourself that you would wait to do it 'when' only to find that 'when' never came. So here's everything you ever wanted and never got."

That imagery woke me up y'all. That was enough for me to start doing the things I thought I never could and the things I thought I was never good enough for. That's when I started making a list and among the many items on that list was one simple, yet important thing to me: drive around Los Angeles in a convertible.

A few years later during my first visit to LA, I fearfully rented a Chevy Camaro. I picked up the car, yet somehow I was still afraid to let the top down. "Am I worthy of driving something that I've labeled as a privilege and above me? What would come next after accomplishing this goal? How would people perceive me?" All of these questions kept the top up.

I called my best friend Ashley and told her about my feelings. As always with an understanding and gentle approach she said to me, "Dominique, if you don't let that damn top down!" She talked me through how foolish I'd be to have come all that way and not do something as simple as push a button. Not to mention the regret I'd have to live with.

I heard every word she said then decided to take a nap, because sometimes all you need to do is go to sleep and start over when you wake up. I told you upfront the difference a morning makes. And my morning was around 5 o'clock in the afternoon when I got up and prepared myself to meet a few friends.

I grabbed the keys, pulled out of the garage, found a spot on a side street, and I let the top down. By the time I reached the next stop sign, I had put on my sunglasses, turned up my Spotify playlist, and fully owned my experience of driving a convertible. For the remainder of the trip I never got in the car without riding with the top down.

That feeling of experiencing what I never thought I could is the same feeling I want for you. Write that book. Go on that vacation. Buy those red bottoms. Go see a Broadway musical. Ride with the top down. Trust that within your lifetime you deserve to experience everything you've ever wanted. Live your life to the fullest, so that you can die empty.

Challenge:

Enjoy your life! Every moment of it. Trust God and do the things that you feel you're not good enough to do. Do them and prove yourself wrong. Live with no regrets and know that you are worthy of everything you desire.

7 I've Been to the Mountaintop

Hands down, Dr. Martin Luther King Jr. is my favorite historical figure of all time. The night before he was murdered, Dr. King gave a speech. Not about a dream he had, but a preview of a coming attraction. The title of that speech? "I've Been to the Mountaintop."

One of the most well-known tourist attractions in Los Angeles, California is Runyon Canyon. At least according to my Instagram feed it is (lol). Videos of people hiking up paved paths, laughing, enjoying nature and the picturesque views of the city from the top of the mountain are what come to mind when I think of this landmark. This experience was one that I wanted for myself. I wanted the mountain top view.

So during my first visit to LA, I checked online and saw that the trails open at sunrise (humph). There goes that "Good Morning" again (lol). The next day - just before 6 a.m. - I got in my car, turned on the GPS, drove to a small dusty parking lot and started on a trail. I immediately noticed that the path around me was all dirt, full of rocks and bushes - nothing like the photos I'd seen on Instagram.

Walking through the only gap in the fence, I hiked the first slope which led me to an opening. From here I could see parts of the city, the canyon, houses and a single landing along the trail. I also saw a few people moving about the canyon. The landing looked to be a good distance away; however, it was the only lookout point I could see and it appeared to have a better view. So I started on my way up.

Upon reaching the landing I saw more of the city. The view was beautiful. I felt accomplished. I'd reached my goal. I hiked Runyon Canyon. I could have gone home; however, I saw another lookout point fixated on what appeared to be a higher plateau. I looked back to see how far I'd come and decided that I could go a little higher.

Now let me tell you, the second landing provided a view that was even better than the first. This time I could see even more of the city. I also saw the paved trail from Instagram and the other people walking it (lol). I didn't mind though, because I had taken the trail less traveled and survived it. Just as I was thinking that it was time to head back to the car, I noticed a third point.

Unlike the previous two, this one was lower. Yet for some reason, I still wanted to see what view it had to offer. I looked back and saw how far up I had hiked. While looking ahead, I got to thinking how crazy I must appear to have reached such a high only to realize that I would gain the view I wanted if I lost the height I had climbed. Laughing at this thought, I made up my mind to go for it.

Sure enough the third lookout point gave me everything I'd hoped it would. I saw the city uninterrupted. It was beautiful. It was fulfilling. I was fulfilled.

At that moment I was reminded that sometimes we gotta lose to win again. C'mon now Fantasia. To others the third point could have been deemed a step down from all of the success that I had gained in climbing up. However, that downgrade gave me the view I wanted. You see, the goal wasn't to climb the highest mountain. My goal was to see Los Angeles in all of its glory. It took me going up just to come down but nevertheless, I got the view I wanted.

We often set goals in life and as we reach them, we realize that it's not the end goal we wanted. So what do we do? We pick a new destination that gets us closer to the end goal. Sometimes you may have to take what others may consider as a step back and that's alright. Not everyone has the foresight to see what you see. Just remember; what others may perceive as a loss could be the best decision for you to reach your ultimate goal.

Unlike Dr. King's speech, my mountain top experience didn't apex with the gratification I gained at the top of a mountain. Mine came as I went from mountain top to mountain top. Dr. King got to peek into the future and saw that the goal was attainable. I took a look back at my journey and saw the same.

wisDOM:

Stop expecting your journey to look like someone else's. What may look like a loss to others could be the biggest gain of your life. Remember, it's the experience that makes the view that much better.

8 Success Is in the Eye of the Beholder

We've all heard the phrase "beauty is in the eye of the beholder." Well somewhere in life I realized that the same applies to success. As I started to understand that I was created to do me and that I was the only person who was equipped to be successful at it; I resolved that it was always up to me to define my own success.

Often we rank success according to our own expectations or what we've seen others do. With that comes a notion that one person's level of success is better than another's and that's not true. Taking a look at the people I've surrounded myself with, I've realized that we are all very much successful in our own right. Reason being is because we've all set different goals and reached them. I believe that success is determined by whether or not you reach your goal; not by how well you match someone else's accomplishments. Go with me if you will.

If your goal was to be Michael Jordan and you ended up being Michael B. Jordan, then guess what? You failed, my friend (lol). Don't get me wrong, you've clearly reached an impressive level of success as an actor; the problem is your goal was to be the GOAT in basketball. You feel me? Aight, a little extreme, I know. Let's go with a more relatable example.

Think of success in the context of traditional education. Let's imagine two students in high school, Johnny and Bobby. Johnny's goal is to graduate college and Bobby's goal is to graduate high school. If Johnny and Bobby graduate high school and only Johnny goes on to graduate college, which one is successful? Allow me to answer that for you: both of them. Because they both reached their respective goals. The same is true when examining levels of success within our families.

My grandparents' level of success meant working a blue collar job for 40 plus years with a promise of a retirement check. My parents viewed success as going to college and securing a job in their chosen field. My generation's general definition of success seems to include working a job that allows time and money for creative satisfaction. Needless to say, the goals and level of success changed with each generation, yet each generation can be considered successful because they each accomplished what they set out to do.

Now, I can't do all of this talk about success without mentioning its twin, failure. For years we have been taught that if you don't succeed then you have failed. Even earlier in this section I stated that not reaching a goal means you have failed. But failing does not make you a failure, giving up does. Even when you think you've lost, you've actually learned. You've learned what doesn't work and that's why some people seem to never "fail." They just live, learn and apply it all moving forward.

Get this in your spirit, success is determined by whether or not you reach your goal, not whether you can match someone else's accomplishments. We each define success differently and in doing so we help redefine what it means to be successful. I guess what I'm attempting to say is success and failure are in the eyes of the beholder.

wisDOM:

You are successful when you reach **YOUR** goals. Don't let other's success define you. You define it.

9 Because I Said So

To Courtney Stephens and Baby Girl

Hands down the one thing I hated growing up was to hear Chell say, "Because I said so." It irked the shit out of me! Like, why do parents think that statement is the end all, be all? Are you saying this because you feel like I can't handle the truth or comprehend the full reasoning behind your directive? Forget that, show me some proof to substantiate your reasoning why it has to be this way.

Don't you look at me in that tone of voice. I wanted answers and being a reason seeking child, you know what I did. I questioned my momma every time. "Why?" "Why?" "Why?" And I kept asking "Why?" "Why?" "Why?" until she threatened to whoop me (lol). I was bad as hell y'all.

Recently I was FaceTiming my 25-year-old cousin Courtney. On my mother's mother's side of the family, I am the youngest in my generation and Courtney is the oldest in the next. So we've developed this "Big-Little Cuz" relationship. Any who, while catching up, the financial hardships of being a single mother to her one-year-old daughter London came up.

Let me just say that I respect anyone who has dedicated their time to raising any number of children. Especially if they did it alone. Attempting to finish college, working one job while looking for another and still make sure that your child has food to eat and clothes to wear while coordinating drop offs and pick-ups… is a lot for anyone. All this to say, I commend Courtney for taking ownership of her situation and working to better it for her daughter.

Adding to the challenges, Courtney also found herself

having to figure out how to navigate a romantic relationship turned co-parenting situationship. This particular day was just one of those days. The girl was sick and tired of being sick and tired. Courtney was looking for answers on how to make it all work and was coming up empty. As always, during our conversations we tend to pour into each other. It's just in our nature.

Standing in her kitchen with her head down washing dishes, Courtney said, "I don't know what to do. Money is tight. Working from home ain't working. School is kickin' my ass. I've tried the government. I've spoken to my parents. I've talked to London's daddy. I don't know what else to do. Why does it have to be this hard?" Feeling and seeing her frustration pouring out, I asked a simple question. "Did you ask Jesus?"

Courtney stopped. Raised her head. Then looked at the phone and said, "You know what? I haven't." We looked at each other as if the answer was sitting right in our faces the whole time. I then warned her, "Ask Him, just don't get mad at the answer. Cause if your God is anything like my God, He may not tell you. And if He does answer, you may get a, 'Because I Said So'."

You see as I've gotten older, I've begun to understand that I don't need to know everything. It's like when you see a group of people running. No need to ask questions, you just take off in the same direction (lol). You'll find out why in the end. And sometimes that's the best way to move through life.

Asking "Why?" derives from a lack of knowledge and also demonstrates a lack of trust. Not so much in the directive but in the director. Let me help you out. Trust is not found in knowing every detail in the direction; it's found in the one giving the direction. Because I trust you, I trust what you're telling me.

Now I see why my Momz frustration after I asked "Why?" resulted in the saying , "because I said so. " Just like me, Courtney realized that she didn't always need to know why. Yes, sometimes not knowing makes us lose trust in the directions given; but, a "because I said so" from a trusted source is all the confirmation we need.

wisDOM:

Not knowing is sometimes the best position to be in. Learn to trust the directive because you trust the director.

10 Accuracy Over Speed

To Mrs. Peggy M. Garner

"Settle down now class. You are about to take a three minute timed writing. You will not be typing for speed. You will be typing for accuracy. Type at a pace that is comfortable for you and never give up accuracy for speed. Now check your machines. Make sure your machines are set at 12-point font. Double spaced. Have you tabbed over? You will start your lines like they start in the text and you will end your lines like they end in the text. You will end them exactly the way they end. Don't start until I tell you to start and stop immediately when I tell you to stop. Hands in position. Eyes on copy. Ready. Begin."

One word: INTENSE. Mrs. Peggy McGraw Garner - a former high school typing and accounting teacher at Childersburg High School - was hands down one of the most memorable educators in the Talladega County school system. Sitting in her class taught me that I could always get it right if I followed instructions. Granted, I haven't always followed instructions (lol).

I've always been the type to want things right and right now. I like to think of myself as an... impatient perfectionist. Somehow, the combination of these two character traits never seems to serve me well. I've always talked too fast and used the wrong verb tense. I've walked too fast and in the wrong direction. And I have moved too fast and made more mistakes than I'd like to admit.

Recently I had a taste for my Granny's sour cream pound cake. I was scheduled to go to an event later that day;

however, I could not shake the craving. So at the last minute I decided to bake this cake. In a haste, I ran to the grocery store to purchase the ingredients then headed home to start baking. After putting the cake in the oven, I realized I had forgotten to add the sour cream! My heart dropped. I'd baked this cake several times before and I've never left out an ingredient.

Disgusted with myself, I just keep looking at the unopened container on the counter. Then it hit me. I was staring at cream cheese. I had bought the wrong ingredient to begin with. I was in such a hurry while at the store that I had picked up the cream cheese that's needed for the icing on Granny's red velvet cake.

I immediately started to laugh out loud. Now what kind of mess would I have made if I had put the cream cheese in the pound cake? I just looked up and thanked God for protecting me from that mistake. So what was I to do next? I did what any normal person would do. I went back to the store after my event and bought the ingredients for the red velvet cake and baked it the next day (lol).

In life we want to get things done and get them done fast. We are all anxious to mark things off of our to-do lists and if we're being honest, we will rush or cut corners just to say that we are done. Hell, I'm guilty of it myself. However, in focusing on speed we often sacrifice accuracy and when we realize that we've gone nowhere fast, we see that short cuts only work until they don't.

Messing up Granny's recipe reminded me of the lessons Mrs. Garner taught in her classroom. In life, just like during Mrs. Garner's typing test, we can't use the backspace key. We can't delete the words we've spoken. We can't get back the time we've wasted or take the cream cheese out of the sour cream pound cake. It's always better to slow down and get it right the first time. We have to consciously value accuracy over speed.

wisDOM:

Trust the timing of your life. Arriving earlier is not always best if you compromise arriving correctly.

11 Don't Yuck My Yum

To Bryson Rose

We all have that one friend that has an opinion about everything that we do. If y'all going out to eat, they have to voice their opinion about what's on your plate. If you tell them about a new fictional movie you want to see, they start talking about how fake it is. And let's not even mention going shopping together. You can't pick up anything without a comment about how they would never! Listen, if you don't have a friend like that, check yourself. You just might be that friend (humph).

Here's a self-test for you. Do you question in disgust what your friends find pleasurable? Have you turned up your nose at something new that your crew wanted to do? Do you start your replies with an unsolicited, "Well if I were you, I would…?" If you answered yes to any of these questions, then I hate to break it to you, but you are that friend.

Don't be mad. Hell, I'm guilty my damn self. I know I've shown my disdain for my friend's love of 1982 sci-fi movies. Like for real, for real. I don't get it. They are not entertaining to me, and I legitimately do not understand how they could possibly be entertaining for anyone else. Any who, I digress (lol). Whenever I find myself feeling like that toward someone else, I'm instantly reminded of something I heard my frat brother Bryson Rose say.

In a culture where we've made it acceptable to express criticism of others for enjoying what brings them joy, I first heard Bryson put it this way, "Don't Yuck My Yum." Now my Brodie isn't the author of this quote, but when he said it, he put a little stank on that 'yuck' and I felt that thang deep in my chakra.

All Bryson was saying is that there are different strokes for different folks. If you don't like it, cool. Just don't knock me because I do. Keep ya little salty comments to yourself if it's not your flavor of Kool-Aid.

Speaking of food – I look at life like a buffet. There are several menu options available to suit a plethora of palettes. I'll let you in on a little secret – the best thing about a buffet is you can put what you want on your plate and leave what you don't for someone else.

If corn pudding ain't your thing, leave it for someone else. If reality TV isn't for you, leave it for someone else. If potato salad with grapes and raisins ain't allowed on your plate, leave it for someone else. If hair relaxers don't fit your style, leave it for someone else. If chitlins funk up your nostrils, then leave it for someone else.

Moment of honesty? Growing up I ate chitlins, I ain't even gonna lie. Granny would get that red bucket with the white top every Thanksgiving and sometimes on Easter. If you're not familiar with this unique delicacy, chitlins are pig intestines. Yuuup. Some eat them with hot sauce, some eat them plain. I used to eat them with ketchup. And if we're keeping it real, some of you just yucked what used to be my yum.

See that's what I'm talking about. I personally haven't

eaten them in years, yet I have no reason to now look down on those who still do. Just because it's no longer my thing doesn't mean that it shouldn't be anyone's thing and the same goes for you.

The old folks used to say, "If you can't say anything nice, then don't say anything at all." Just keep your thoughts to yourself. No one wants to hear that their choices don't meet your standards. So what if it's not your jush; not yucking someone else's yum shows respect for their choices. And if asked for an opinion, just tell them, "If you like it, I love it."

wisDOM:

If we're being honest, you like some shit that others would find repulsive. So let these folks live. You may not like their choices, however you can respect their decisions.

12 Go, You'll Be Fine

*To my mentor and chosen mother —
the late Mrs. Corine Woods*

July 2012. Sitting in the parking deck preparing to visit my mentor and chosen mother; my nerves were getting the best of me. Here I am with something I had to tell her yet wasn't sure how she would take it.

Ironically, my chosen sister and fellow mentee also had news for Momma and was equally nervous. I looked over and asked, "Tash, you ready to do this?" "As ready as you are Baby Boy," she replied. We got out the car and walked through the automatic doors. Reaching the front desk, we asked for the room of Mrs. Corine Woods.

Upon approaching the hospital room, I heard laughter. Momma was surrounded by her daughter, LaRessa, a few of her siblings and friends. In true Southern hospitality, Tasha and I greeted everyone in the room, regardless of whether we knew them or not.

We each took a turn leaning over the hospital bed to give our mentor a hug. She was so happy to see us. You could just feel it.

Although laying in the bed, Momma still took the personal privilege to get everyone's attention before running down the list of accomplishments of Tasha and I. Blushing, we took it. We stood there awkwardly as we had done so many times before receiving the praise from a woman who had invested so much into so many.

After she wrapped up her introductions, one of Momma's sisters exclaimed, "Oh, so these are the two! She talks about y'all all the time. Y'all are family. Have a seat!"

Following instructions, we got as comfortable as our nerves would allow at the foot of the hospital bed. Then everyone decided to leave the room so that we could get some alone time with Momma.

Because it was more comfortable for Momma to lay flat, she fixed her eyes on the ceiling. After a few moments of casual conversation, Tasha looked at me as to nudge me to go first. I took a deep breath and said, "Momma, I have something to tell you."

Not taking her eyes off of the ceiling, she waited for me to continue. Nervously, I blurted it out, "I'm moving to New York." She flinched. My whole world stopped. To quickly break the silence, I said, "I got accepted into NYU for graduate school. I'll be leaving in seven weeks and I'm not sure if I can do it."

Holding my breath in anticipation for a response, it seemed as if time stood still. Then she moved. Lowering her chin towards her feet to look at me, our eyes met. She parted her lips and said, "Go, you'll be fine." Returning her head back to her pillow she repeated, "Yeah, you'll be fine."

I exhaled. Gaining confidence from what she had just witnessed, Tasha began to tell Momma that she had been accepted into Meharry Medical College and that she was finally starting med school in the fall. Momma chuckled. Trying to compose herself, she put one hand over her mouth as she always did when laughing. Not saying a word, Momma's pride and joy exuded from her and filled the room.

We sat and talked for nearly another hour before anyone else entered the room. As more visitors began to arrive, Tasha and I decided that we would give up our seats to those just coming in. Again Momma silenced the room to announce the news we gave her. Everyone was so happy. The many congratulations were genuine and heartfelt. We each gave Momma one more hug and a kiss goodbye.

About two weeks later, I received a call that Momma had transitioned. Sad, hurt, confused yet comforted, I moved through the next few weeks holding on to the last bit of advice she gave me.

While in grad school, I faced several obstacles. Many days I wanted to give up. Some days I actually did. Yet, I knew that getting knocked down and staying down wasn't an option. So I pushed and pushed and pushed some more until I got through.

On May 20, 2015, I woke up, got dressed and headed to Yankee Stadium to be conferred the Masters of Science in Integrated Marketing with a focus in Brand Management degree that I had worked so hard to attain. While in the car I looked up to the sky. With the sun shining bright in my eyes, I whispered, "Momma, you were right."

If that wasn't enough, on that same day two years later my sister became Dr. Tasha Garrett, MD. The moral of the story is: regardless of what you feel, no matter how scared you are of the unknown, GO! If not for you then for people who have poured so much in you. I promise; just go, you'll be fine.

wisDOM:

In starting anything, the fear you may feel may cripple you but with every step you take, you will feel more and more confident about your journey. All you have to do is go. You'll be fine.

13 8 Tracks, CDs, MP3s

To Pastor Clarence Woodward

I am a firm believer that change won't change until we change. No doubt we are creatures of habit. We naturally gravitate towards what we are used to.

If I'm being honest, I'm guilty of resisting change myself. When I look back over situations I've encountered during my life, I can clearly see that in some cases, change was necessary and in some it was an option. Take whooping children for example. I got my ass whooped as a kid so I think whooping ass is an option for all kids. Hell, I turned out alright.

With that said, I do believe that every child does not need whoopings to be taught a lesson. My brother Jarrod was one of them. If you looked at him wrong, he would straighten up and walk right. Me on the other hand, if you said you were going to get the belt then I would respond with, "Well, let me see it" (lol). Even after seeing the belt I would only calm down long enough for you to get distracted by something else and then I was back to my regular scheduled shenanigans.

All I'm saying is whooping ass still works and all old methods should not be thrown away in new times. Certain things served us well in the past and they might still serve a purpose today. For all other things, outside of sparing the rod, let's consider updating our approach to match our goals (lol).

As the generations grow and adapt, so should our methods. However, even in changing our methods, the message should remain the same. Just like in technology and music. The way in which we consume music has evolved yet we still enjoy our favorite tunes.

From 8 tracks we move next to cassettes. Then there were CDs followed by wave files and MP3s. Now music is stored on an online database and just streamed anytime we want to hear it. If how we listen to music has evolved over time, then so must how we engage with others.

Back home in Alabama, my pastor Clarence Woodward used to put it like this, "You can't win a CD generation using 8 Tracks. It's out of date." And I couldn't agree more. Old ways won't always open new doors. Hell, even God switched it up a few times.

In the book of Isaiah, the prophet writes to the people of God who are in captivity in Babylon. He says, *"Forget the former things; do not dwell on the past. See, I am doing a new thing…"* - Isaiah 43:18-19 NIV.

What He was saying was to not limit future possibilities because you're expecting me [God] to move in the same way I did the last time. To be honest, God never went about things the same way twice. He can't be put in a box. He's too complex for that.

Alright, Alright, Alright. If God switched up his approach, then maybe I can evolve my notions around whopping ass (lol). All I'm saying is, it's okay to remember what was done in the past as long as we don't get fixated on how it was done. It won't hurt if we don't do it like Granny used to do it. It's alright to change up the method as long as the message remains the same. Nothing stays the same year after year; so neither should we.

wisDOM:

Change is inevitable. So embrace it. As long as the message or outcome remains the same, do things however you feel. Just be efficient and effective.

14 Do It Anyhow

*To my grade school besties -
Takova Wallace-Gay and Kelli Owens*

I made history y'all! In 2004 I became the fourth Black person and second Black male ever in history to become the drum major of the Childersburg High School Tiger Marching Band.

For my first game as drum major, my entire support system was there. I'm talking my parents, older brother, pastor and his wife, church members, aunties, uncles, cousins… literally, all of my people came just to see me, and y'all, I was nervous as hell.

As the second quarter came to a close, the band and I prepared to take the field. In what seemed like an out of body dream, I found my best friends and confessed how scared and underprepared I felt. Takova, along with my other best friend Kelli, quickly reassured me that I was going to do just fine. Honestly, they had more confidence in me than I had in myself at that moment. Swallowing my nerves, I rallied the troops and took our place on the backside of the football field.

I remember the bright lights illuminating the empty field seated at my feet. The crowd's excitement radiating toward me began to collect in the pit of my stomach. I called the band to attention using my whistle. Then gave the signal for the matching cadence.

Tap...Tap...Tap...Tap

As I moved across the field with the band at my heels, I

could see the crowd rise to their feet, yet my ears could hear nothing but the rhythm of the drums. I made it to my mark and turned to face the band as I had rehearsed so many times before. The cadence stopped. Shoulders clinched, I got even more scared. I'm talking down right fearful.

With my back to the crowd and facing about 100 band members, I searched for comfort. Scanning the line in front of me, I found and made eye contact with Takova. I mouthed, "I can't do it". She responded, "You got this!" followed by a slight head nod. With my body frozen in fear, my eyes bucked and terror written on my face I shook my head in opposition. That's when I heard the words over the stadium speakers that I once longed for but was now dreading, *"Drum Major, Dominique Lee, Is Your Band Ready?"*

I took a deep breath. As I spun around to respond, my face turned from fearful to confident. Power exuded from my now relaxed shoulders. With my head held high I began to move. My body did what came naturally. I tossed the baton in the air knowing that it would come back down. As it landed safely in one hand, the other rose to my brow to salute the crowd.

It all flowed with ease. It all went just the way I had planned it. As I exhaled, my hearing returned to a thundering roar from the crowd. From that moment on I was fearless. I did it! With fear in my eyes and uncertainty in my heart I did it. Not only did I go on to lead the band for the following nine games, I maintained my position for the following year.

And every game I went out and gave the people a show.

Sometimes people may have more faith in your abilities than you do and that's alright. Just never settle on becoming your own roadblock on the way to your goals and dreams. I don't care if you feel unqualified, unprepared or undeserving; do it anyhow. Scared, crying, tired or full of fear; do it anyhow. If it requires you to go against the crowd, to move in silence or to step outside of your comfort zone and out on faith; do it anyhow. Not doing will fill you with years of shouldas, couldas, and wouldas. So do your future self a favor now and do it anyhow.

wisDOM:

There is no need to fear when you're facing something new. Yeah, you may be afraid, but do it afraid. Do it anyhow.

15 You Take Care Now

I know I'm not the only one who, as a child, would eavesdrop on their parents' phone calls. Many times I'd use context clues to figure out who was on the other end. Sometimes it sounded like a one-way conversation and other times it seemed to be a banter back and forth. Regardless, the call typically ended with an "Alright. You take care now."

"You take care now." What does that really mean? Does it mean to eat right, exercise and drink plenty of water? Maybe it serves as a reminder to give attention to the situations that matter most and maintain a level of joy, peace and love.

Three decades later, I still don't know (lol). Shid, what did you expect? I can't have all the answers (humph). One thing I do know is that self-care and taking care of yourself are two different things.

Within our culture, there's an unspoken idea that mental and emotional health comes second to financial health and relationship obligations. I must admit that I've fallen victim to this notion myself. I assumed the mindset that taking care of certain necessities was my top priority. I was determined, with God's help, to have food on my table, clothes on my back and a roof over my head. C'mon now church (lol). In fact, I was so serious about this thing that it even got to the point where if I asked for help, my family knew I had already exhausted all of my resources. This became my modus operandi or mode of operating - also known as my M.O.

For months I would work as much overtime as possible.

I would settle for a laptop I didn't want as opposed to the one I had saved up for just so that I would not appear to be irresponsible to my friends. Hell, at one point, I even convinced myself that attending family milestone events was the only vacation I was entitled to have. The major drawback to all of this was that I was taking care of myself and being there for other people at the expense of my own wellbeing.

You see, I was good, but I wasn't happy. Not quite depressed, just stuck in a survival mentality because I refused to become one of those people who always needed help. I thought the best way for me to take care of others was to take care of myself. And while, to some degree, this was true, I took the notion too far.

I was so caught up in ensuring that I had a life to live that I never lived the life I had. I was only taking care of myself while neglecting my own self-care.

What is self-care? Essentially, self-care is taking care of one's mental and emotional state in an attempt to better one's overall health. I'm talking about maintaining a level of peace, loving deeply, focusing on physical health, ensuring a proper work-life balance and accepting yourself for everything you are while releasing the anguish toward everything you're not. Studies have shown that bringing these areas of life into focus helps with productivity, enhances self-esteem, boosts the immune system and improves overall physical health. Don't believe me? Google it.

It took some time and a whole lot of conscious effort, but I've learned to balance taking care of myself with self-care. Today, I intentionally make time to be silent, to treat myself to things I like and make time for those I love.

You and I are each responsible for every aspect of our lives and that includes our mental and emotional health. Taking care of ourselves and self-care looks differently for each of us; however, both are essential to living a fulfilling holistic life. So now, when someone says, "You take care now," make sure you do just that.

Challenge:

Be intentional about balancing taking care of yourself with self-care. Focus on you in your pursuit of a holistic life because YOU are essential to your journey.

16 The Price of Glory Is High

*To Randy Ferino Wayne Jr. and
the Mighty Marching Hornets of Alabama State University*

Singing: *"Early in the morning"* - (echo) *"in the morning"* - *"before I eat my breakfast, I gotta get up"* – (echo) *"to get what"* - *"to get down. I gotta get up"* – (echo) *"to get what"* - *to get down"* – (echo) *"I can't hear you!"*

If you went to a Historically Black College or University, then this song, or at least some version of it, was probably your alarm clock during orientation week. As a new student staying on campus at Alabama State University, I woke up to this song I know the entire first week of school. The Mighty Marching Hornets singing while making their way past King Hall at the crack of dawn became my norm and I loved every moment of it.

As I mentioned in the section "Do It Anyhow", I marched in my high school band. What I didn't mention was that I used to mimic the Mighty Marching Hornets – to the best of my ability. Even to the point where everyone knew I was bound to become a Marching Hornet… Everyone, that is, but me.

By the time I enrolled at Alabama State as a transfer student, I'd already convinced myself that the price of glory was high, and my credit couldn't get it. As a matter of fact, that's the band's motto; "The Price of Glory is High." And one person I knew who was on top of his payment plan was my roommate: Randy Ferino Wayne Jr. Yes, when I introduce him, I say his whole name (lol). Randy was a rising junior and third year Marching Hornet who at the time was auditioning to be a drum major.

Randy was more than dedicated to the band and the work required to receive the coveted leadership position. I witnessed him getting up early every morning and coming in late in the evenings. When he did have a break, he would either sleep or help band members learn the Bama State Style of marching. From summer camp into the first week of classes, Randy focused on leading by example.

About two weeks into the school year, we learned that Randy did not get one of the five drum major positions. Hurt, yet not defeated, Randy remained faithful to the band. He picked up his saxophone and marched the entire season. For that year and the following, Randy still got up early in the morning and worked late into the night. He knew that every Marching Hornet had a price to pay. Not just the drum majors.

What's the lesson here? Look at you asking the right questions (lol). We often hold those in leadership positions to a higher standard than those who are not. I can agree that there is a greater responsibility when being a leader; however, the same level of dedication, effort and attention to detail is the charge for anyone associated; even those not in leadership positions.

Just like Randy, we should all remember that a lack of title does not give us an excuse to do less. The CEO and the janitor both have a responsibility to be great and greatness comes with a price. We all have the responsibility to execute at a certain level of excellence and contribute our best so that glory can be attained. Now if you don't want to pay the cost, then I suggest you find another band to play in where the price is in your budget.

Challenge:

Even when you feel like your role is small compared to others, make your role big to you. Give all you've got and remember: The Price of Glory is High.

17 Eating Is a Hard Habit to Break

To Cannon Kent

I don't know about you, but I love to eat. Been doing it since day one and for some reason I just can't stop! I've had the roof of my mouth burned. Had food leave me with a bad aftertaste. Even ate some shit that's made me sick. Yet, I've never willingly missed a meal.

The same can be said about my desire to work in entertainment. Watching artists on TV as a kid lead me to studying the inner workings of the industry as an undergrad student. And might I add that Alabama State University is the only Historically Black College or University to have a degree granting program in music business. Get into it. But I digress.

While in undergrad, a few of my major classes included copyright laws of intellectual property, concert promotion, artist management and contract negotiations. Another requirement was to spend two semesters interning within the industry. At the time, every student had to secure their own internships and get approval from the then department head, Dr. William Ashbourne.

After a little work, I landed a summer internship in Atlanta with the Southeastern Promotional Director of Atlantic Records. Cannon Kent literally took a chance on ya boy and put me to work. My trial assignment was to be an elevator attendant during DJ Drama's "Gangsta Grillz Vol. 2" album release event. Yuuup, that's right! I stood in the lobby and sent the elevator to the 3rd floor every time someone came in. Do you think I minded? Hell nawl! I was just happy to be in the building.

After that event my day-to-day tasks grew to updating radio directories and mailing out CDs. Then I graduated to tracking radio airplay and preparing reports for Cannon and her meetings. Occasionally I got to put my event planning skills to use by curating album release events and radio meet and greets for Laura Izabor, Sean Paul and Trey Songz just to name a few.

At the end of the summer I returned back to school; however, I wasn't fulfilled. You see, I had gotten a taste of the life I wanted and now simply studying the industry wasn't enough. I emailed Cannon and expressed my interest in assisting her throughout the school year. Sure enough whenever an event came up, Cannon reached out to see if I was available and I took her up on every offer.

Being a dedicated hard worker with a "get it done by any means necessary" mentality, earned me another summer of interning with Cannon. By this time, she knew I was hungry for the experience and not thirsty for the fame. Cannon saw that I was hooked, and I wanted to do the work. So, this time around, I was even more involved. Not only did she seek out my recommendations, but she also let me take the lead on a few initiatives. She even openly gave me credit while on a department conference call with the other regional reps and SVPs in New York City.

As if that wasn't enough, Cannon gave me the opportunity to travel and work dates in her market during

Trey Songz' first headlining tour. Not every intern got this opportunity. Now let me make this clear, none of my expenses were covered nor was this a paid internship. But because I had already gotten a taste and was hungry for more, I covered my own expenses to work these shows. Yuuup (in my Trey Songz voice), and it was one of the best decisions I've made to date.

Since then I've never not worked in entertainment. I've started careers in other industries; however, I've always kept a nonpaying role, a freelance position, a barter agreement or something working with musical artists and their art.

And the same can happen for you. Once you've had a taste of your passion you will find ways to satisfy your hunger. And yes, you may likely have to start at the bottom and pay your own way a time or two. You may get burned, have a nasty experience and even get sick of it all. However, none of this will stop you from eating, because no matter what, you will never get enough. Cannon gave me the first taste of my dreams all those years ago; from then on, eating has been a hard habit to break.

wisDOM:

Stay hungry and feed your passion. Once you get a taste, you'll understand that eating is a hard habit to break.

18
I Got You

There are three little words that when spoken by the right person can change your life. Most think those words are "I love you." Some may argue that it's "Are you hungry?" I, on the other hand, believe "I got you" carries the most weight.

Let's get one thing straight: actions always speak louder than words. We've all had people to say things and then not back it up. Some of them knew from jump they couldn't keep their word. I ain't going to talk about ya flaky friends right now; but the point I'm making is that the follow-through is essential to validating any statement.

Now back to these three little words. In my opinion "I got you" crosses the spectrum of relationships. We've heard hard core street guys on television say it to their partners in crime as well as when two lovers who are building trust in their relationship. Let's not forget that "I got you" is comforting to the soul when we hit up the party promoter to not stand in line at the club or pay when we get to the door. I'm just saying (lol).

"I got you" carries so much weight and rightfully so. To be verbally told by someone that you are depending on, that they "got you" allows you the space to breathe a sigh of relief. The phrase when backed up by actions says I love you, I'm with you, no worries, you can depend on me. It literally means I GOT YOU. And the best voice to hear this from is God.

I don't know about you but, God has a funny way of showing me that He got me. In the summer of 2015, I was fired from my part-time job and heard God say, "I got you." Just weeks prior, I had been told by a major record label VP that he wanted me as his assistant, so I didn't take being let go personal.

Working in entertainment has always been my career field of choice. The year before, I interviewed for the same position and was passed over. So when I was told that he should have hired me in the first place, I knew he had confidence in me and that I was the best fit for the role. For six years I had pursued a career in the music industry, and it finally looked as if it was going to happen.

After months of several interviews, countless phone calls and numerous emails, I received a call from human resources saying that they thought that my interest lied in other areas and that they were moving forward with another candidate. I was pissed, hurt, and confused.

By this time, I had been waiting three months to start work. I was unemployed, overdrawn in my checking account and emotionally drained. The only thing I could do was trust God and start looking for a job. So, that's what I did.

Three years later, while working in advertising and freelancing in the music business through my own company - 8th Wonder, I ended up meeting and befriending a guy who worked for that label. Of course, I asked how he liked the company and casually inquired how that VP was doing. He replied, "Oh, they let him go right after I started in 2015."

You can imagine my shock. I then shared my story and he informed me that the assistant they ended up hiring started her first day without a boss and she had to be reassigned. He said, "Be happy you didn't get that job."

At that moment I heard God say, "See, I told you I got you."

That's what I'm talking about. It wasn't until years later; however, the confirmation came. What appeared to be a missed blessing was actually God's protection from a situation that I was never supposed to be in.

I know God got me. He said that He would never leave nor forsake me and His track record proves that. Following His lead, we as humans should do the same. When you hear me or anyone say "I got you," check the follow through. If the walk aligns with the talk, rest assured that you're in good hands.

Challenge:

Trust that when someone says "I got you" that they got you unless or until proven otherwise.

19 The Waiting Room

Welcome to the waiting room. This is the place in your life where you feel like you're stuck between the past and the future. What you want to do and what you have to do. A feeling of hope matched with a face full of realities. This period in your life feels like you're running on a treadmill. Your feet are moving and your heart is racing, yet you are going nowhere.

The waiting room can be a dark and cold place. Be it in our careers, love lives or in our spiritual walks. But, no worries. We've all been in this space before and some of us; multiple times. So don't be surprised or discouraged when you find yourself in this space more than once in your life - you're not alone.

Producer, writer and actor James Bland once described the waiting room as a plane attempting to land. I liked that analogy, so I did a little more research and took it a bit further.

As an aircraft approaches an airport, the pilot speaks with a controller who sits high in the towers and controls what happens below on the ground. If the controller tells the pilot "No, you cannot land just yet," then the pilot has to keep circling in the air until permission is given to start the descent. The controller, who sees the bigger picture, can keep that plane circling for such reasons as runway traffic, unsafe weather conditions or a lack of open gates. So the holding pattern is really protection for the pilot and everyone on board.

Can I make it plain for you? God is the controller. You are the pilot. The passengers on the plane are all the people assigned to your life. And the checked bags and carry-ons are all of your gifts and talents. The holding pattern is the waiting room and it's designed to keep you from experiencing a fatal accident. What may appear to be stalling in your life could be protection from something that could take you out.

When I look back over my life I see that what seemed to be a holding pattern at the time was actually a waiting room preparing me for my arrival. Where in many cases, I had the talent to get my foot in the door, I hadn't yet developed the character to keep me in the room. While God was preparing me for what was next, He was also preparing what was next for me.

When I started interning at my second record label, I just knew I was going to turn this internship into a job. One day I walked into the office and the coordinator I was working under had been let go. Her two bosses decided to have me fill in temporarily until they found a permanent replacement.

I just knew this was my chance! For the next month I put my other part-time job on hold and rearranged my schedule to be available before and after regular business hours. I started taking initiative, making my presence known, building a good reputation and showcasing what I brought to the table.

All that to say, I didn't get the job. This didn't feel good.

Another waiting room. After I got out of my feelings, I realized that even without the job, God had given me the tools and insight I needed to grow my own entertainment brand management firm.

What I'm saying to you is, don't get resentful because you're in the waiting room. Don't get mad because you think it's time to land and the controller says, "no, not yet." Trust that this holding pattern is for your own safety. Just like we talked about in a previous section "I got you" - trust that when God got you in the waiting room that He got you, even in the waiting room.

Challenge:

Whatever waiting room or holding pattern you seem to be in, don't become bitter. Develop your character. It won't be long now.

20 I Am...

To Lyndell Pittman

Now don't get it twisted. After reading "Do It Anyhow" you may think that I was and still am forever fearless. Chile Please! I'm a punk in real life. I ain't afraid to admit it (lol).

Many times I punk out when I focus on what I see instead of what I believe. For me, it often takes place in areas where I know my worth and even at my best I still don't measure up based on criteria outlined by someone else. The perfect example took place when I felt it was time to start looking for a new 9-to-5.

After four years in pharmaceutical advertising, I started to get restless and felt that I needed a change. Like many of you, I did what most would do. I updated my resume and applied for jobs I knew I wasn't qualified for (lol).

I also let a few people in my social and professional circles know that I was looking for new employment opportunities. A fraternity brother, Lyndell Pittman, sent me an opening at his job. I reviewed the job description and saw a few responsibilities I felt were above my capabilities; so I didn't apply.

The next week Lyndell was running errands on his lunch break near my office. I offered to step outside to get some air and check in to see how he was doing. During our conversation, he asked me if I applied for the position. Being the honest person I am, I said no and told him the reason why. Right there in the middle of the street outside of my office building, Lyndell Pittman ripped me a new one.

He went off! He didn't care who was watching and I was so embarrassed. Picture two grown ass men on the sidewalk. One [Lyndell] passionately communicating his disappointment in the other. And the other [me] just standing there taking it.

I can't recall all that he said because hell, I was too focused on not being "those people" in front of all of New York City. But I do remember he said that as a man of this fraternity, we do not shy away from opportunities. We rise to meet them.

All I could do was say "okay"; because deep down I knew he was right. Not just as a brother, but as a believer. It wasn't so much about the job as much as it was about what I was subconsciously telling myself.

I'd learned years ago, and had clearly forgotten, that the two most powerful words that we as humans could speak is "I Am". Reason being, whatever we say next defines who we are and shapes who we will become.

You see, in this particular instance I was saying, "I am not qualified. I am not experienced. I am not enough." But after my talk with Lyndell, my "I Ams" changed.

I started saying things like – "I am qualified. I am enough. I am talented. I am a winner. I am successful." And then it spilled over into my personal life.

I started saying, "I am unstoppable. I am confident. I am happy. I am tall enough. I am attractive. I am loved. I am the right size. I am the embodiment of infinite possibilities."

Can I get churchy for a moment? I am **healed**. I am **blessed**. I am **called**. I am **favored**. I am a **conqueror**. I am a **child of the most high**. I am **forgiven**. I am **redeemed**. I am **the head** and not the tail. I am a **lender** and not a borrower. I am **above** and not beneath.

In the third chapter of Exodus, Moses received instructions from God to go to Pharaoh and get the children of Israel out of Egypt. Moses asked God for the name to tell the people who sent him. God replied, *"I am who I am. This is what you are to say to the Israelites: 'I Am has sent me to you.'"* Exodus 3:14 NLT

Picture it, Moses, the one who stuttered, is whom God used to change history. Not only that, God did it using Moses' most prominent weakness; his speech. Where Moses lacked, God picked up the slack. And He does the same for you and I. Even when I'm not, I serve a God that is. God fills in the gap. He is that unexplainable thing that folks just can't seem to put their finger on when they think about me. God is what sets me apart. God is my differentiating factor.

I challenge you, every day when you wake up, look yourself in the mirror and declare your I Ams over your day. And when the world hits you with what you are not, you hit back with, "Oh, but God is".

wisDOM:

God said when you are weak, I am strong. When you are lonely, I am the friend that sticks closer than a brother. When you can't see your way; I am the way, the truth and the light. I am everything you want and everything that you'll need. I am that I Am.

21 Being Willing and Able

Question for you: have you ever set a goal and then in mid pursuit just decided, "Nah, I'm good on that" (lol)? I know I have. And when I do, I realize that the feeling comes from either one of two places. I call it: being willing and able.

The "**Willing**" relates to the mental aspect; or your desires. To complete any task or even make a decision, you have to get your mind right. Being mentally prepared could be checking to make sure your mood is right or ensuring that the task doesn't conflict with your values or natural instincts.

Being "**Able**" correlates to the physical aspect; or your capabilities. In order to do anything, you have to be physically able to do it. Thinking through the physical and sometimes financial aspect of things help to determine if the task is even humanly possible.

The issue starts when we are not willing AND able. You see the word "and"? That means in addition to. Sometimes we are willing to do something, but just not able. And sometimes we are able but not willing. This misalignment is the fundamental problem in some folks' relationships. Aight now! Here we go!

I myself have been guilty of chasing after a love that wasn't both willing and able. Don't look at me funny like you ain't done the same! You know you were pushing up on Cathy or John, whatever your preference, and he or she didn't push back.

Be honest with me, you've been interested in someone who was single on paper, yet their heart and feelings were with their ex. You invested your time and effort to show them how good of a person you were only to find that they "just weren't ready to be in a relationship." Yeah, not willing yet able.

Or maybe you came across someone who was interested in you. They checked off all the boxes on your list. Wanted you and said they loved you but their spouse wanted them (umm hmm). That's what you call willing but not able. Either way you put it, the relationship just wouldn't work. Any who, let me get out of your business and talk about something I'm familiar with: me and my life (lol).

One night I was on a family conference call with Jarrod and Chell. Somehow we got to talking about our goals and what we wanted to accomplish within the coming year. My mother shared that she wanted to expand her beauty salon. Having worked alone in her own shop for some time; she now wanted to have multiple stylists working under her. In addition to employees, she mentioned how she wanted to give young stylists the opportunity to gain real world experience through internships.

Jarrod, being the realist he is, started asking my mother questions about the practicality of her dreams. "What type of hands-on experience will you be able to provide? Where will these students come from? Will this be for class credit? Do you have the space or setup in your current shop to hold the increase in stylists?"

I sat back and listened while they talked through these

questions. After being silent the entire time, my mother inquired my opinion. I could only think of one thing to ask, "Are you willing and able to carry out this dream?"

Uncertain of the question, she asked me to elaborate. I walked her through my explanation of being willing and able and even used examples from my own life. Not long before this conversation, I had a come to Jesus meeting with myself. It was a moment where I took an in-depth look at some of the things I wanted to do in my life. And I realized that for some things, I was either willing but not able, or able and not willing.

Explaining this aloud not only helped me accept my newest epiphany, but also sparked one for my mother. And I want the same thing for you - to understand that both the mental and the physical is needed to bring a dream to fruition. So now here's my challenge to you. Get that thing in your head – the one goal you can't seem to shake – and ask yourself "am I willing AND able?"

Challenge:

Before committing to anything, ask yourself if you are willing and able to see it through; because if you're going to do it, then it's going to take ALL of you.

22 Can You Stand the Rain?

Music is my first love and oftentimes I find new revelations through the lyrics and melodies even if I've heard the song before.

A while ago, I was listening to R&B legends Ralph, Ronnie, Johnny, Ricky and Mike; known as New Edition and the forever classic song they released in the late 80s, written and produced by Jimmy Jam and Terry Lewis titled: "Can You Stand the Rain." You know the words.

"Sunny days, everybody loves them.

Tell me baby can you stand the rain?

Storms will come.

This we know for sure

(This we know for sure)

Can you stand the rain?"

From there my mind traveled to an album cut from the gospel duo Mary Mary called "Dirt". Erica and Tina Campbell said,

"But we all. Need a little bit.

Need a little bit. Need a little bit of dirt to grow

We need a little bit. Need a little bit.

Need a little rain to wash our souls.

We need a little bit. Need a little dirt to grow."

In internalizing these lyrics, I realized that we all need both rain and dirt.

Dirt, although often unwanted, is needed to produce life.

When we understand just how important dirt is in the growth process of plants, we will begin to understand just how significant it is when "dirt is thrown on our names".

Dirt, contrary to popular belief, is full of the things we need. It keeps us grounded and humbled. It teaches us how to push and grow through hardships and setbacks. Maybe, just maybe, at some point in our journey God says you need some fresh nutrients to propel your growth. From where I stand Mary Mary got it right. We absolutely need a little bit of dirt to grow, but what's dirt without rain?

Rain keeps us fresh. Rain clears the air. Rain quenches our thirst and don't act like you've never been thirsty (lol). Rain comes to cool us off when we start to burn out. Rain is essential to the growth process.

Sixty percent of our bodies are made of water and 71 percent of the earth's surface is water-covered. Rain, a major component of the water cycle, is responsible for depositing most of the fresh water on Earth. What this tells me is that rain is the rejuvenating process of filling the very thing that makes up the majority of my being. Both rain and dirt are vital to my existence.

There's an old story about a donkey who fell in an empty well. He found himself so far down in the well that he wasn't able to climb out. A few people walking by heard the donkey and started calling him stupid and saying how he was going to die in the well.

The donkey's owner, who was out looking for him, saw the neighbors crowding around the well. In his attempt to save what belonged to him, the owner started dumping dirt down the well followed by a bucket of rain water. As the dirt and water fell all over the donkey, he shook it off and just stomped its hoofs. The neighbors begin to laugh and say the owner was just as dumb as the donkey. But that didn't stop the owner. He continued to dump dirt and water in the well and the donkey continued to shake it off and stomp its hoofs.

The owner spent hours doing this and in his wisdom knew just how much dirt and how much rain water the donkey could take at once. The donkey, not understanding what his owner was doing, just shook the dirt off and kept packing it under his feet. After a while the neighbors saw that the dry dirt mixed with the rain water packed under the donkey's feet began to harden. Repeating this process built up the bottom of the well and the donkey was able to get out on its own.

What's the moral of the story? God knows just how much dirt and how much rain you can bear. He's already calculated what it will take to get you out of that hole you're in. No matter how much dirt is thrown your way or how much rain is falling in your life, just shake it off and pat it under your feet. Both the rain and the dirt are needed for you to grow.

wisDOM:

Both rain and dirt are needed to grow in life. When people ask, "How can you smile while in the middle of a storm?" or "Why are you not shocked when dirt is thrown your way?" Just reply both are to be expected and that you intend to go through the rain and grow through the dirt.

23 No Worries Step Clap

To my chosen brother and sister - RAII & Whitney

I've had the privilege to work with, befriend and just kick it with some good-hearted people in the entertainment industry. Two of those good people are independent artists who just happen to be husband and wife. Hailing from Chicago, Illinois, RAII and Whitney are two people who can just sang y'all!

You may know them from their audition on season 11 of America's Got Talent, or maybe you've seen them singing behind Alicia Keys, Ed Sheeran, Estelle, Common, and so many others. I'm blessed to know them as my chosen brother and sister, prayer partners and bosses (lol).

Even after touring the world and being on countless stages, there was a point in their careers where they found themselves unemployed for over seven months while living in New York City. Years later, I remember being with them during an interview and hearing RAII talk about how they once shared a $5 chicken box for dinner because that's all they could afford. And Whitney mentioning how she used to put plastic bags in her worn shoes to keep the rain puddles from getting her feet wet. WooLawd! They for sure have some testimonies.

Well one day while in their "Waiting Room" season, these two took their gifts and did what they do best. They created. RAII was in the living room making a track on his laptop. Whitney, hearing the music, danced into the living room with tears in her eyes and her hands lifted up. When she opened her mouth the words, "No worries, we'll get through it all" just flowed out. And just like that their beautiful story of faith-n-work was born.

Sung over an infectious island beat, RAII opens the song by saying,

"You've been fighting, fight on.

You've been trying, keep on.

Don't you let them dim your light.

Shine on, shine on through the night."

The second verse continues the theme of perseverance. Whitney comes in with,

"You've been fighting, keep going.

You've been low so you can go higher.

Don't rush yourself, embrace the preparation.

Let them talk, let them talk,

They don't know how great you are."

If that's not encouraging enough, in the chorus the two say, *"No worries. We'll get through it all."* along with instructions to a victory dance called the "Step Clap."

Now between all the rehearsals, sound checks, live shows and even at home during my personal worship time, I know I've heard this song and done this dance close to a thousand times. But somewhere around the 563rd time, it started to hit a little different.

I realized that the song was about going through trials and situations and the dance was instructions on **how** to go through. As humans, when we hit hard times, we tend to freeze up. We would rather not make a move in fear of making a wrong move. And it's natural. Dark, unsettling and even parallelizing moments can force us to stay in a place that was never created for us to set up residence. Can I help you out though? Whenever you find yourself in these places all you have to do is step and clap.

As simple as it sounds, the song lays it out. What you have to remember is that the step comes before the clap; however, both stepping and clapping are needed for the victory. Y'all, I'm about to make myself happy! Can I make it plain for you? The step represents you putting forth effort to move out of your current situation. The clap represents giving God praise.

When you're walking through the valley of the shadow of death, do just what the song says - take a step and clap. When your money is looking funny and your change is looking strange - take a step and clap. When you've cried your last cry, wipe away the tears - take a step and clap. Look at your neighbor, I don't care if they aren't reading this book, speak life into whatever situation they may feel stuck in and tell them "No Worries, Step Clap."

Challenge:

Go through your valley moments but don't set up shop. Know that you will get through it all. So no worries, just step and clap.

24 Who Yo' Folks?

Growing up in what I affectionately call "the backwoods" of Alabama meant that there was no escaping being recognized by somebody. With no more than 12.5 thousand people living in a small town, there's at most 2 degrees of separation. Somebody went to school with somebody who went to church or worked with my momma, daddy, grandparents, uncles and/or aunts.

And don't let me run into someone at Walmart, because if you want to run into anyone just go to Walmart. A run-in with a high school classmate's parent, who may not recognize me on sight, usually involves a brief exchange of Southern pleasantries and then that one question, "Who yo' folks?"

Having experienced this on several occasions, my response is, "I'm Machelle and Julyan Lee's son." This is often followed by something like, "Oh you're Coke's Boy!" (lol). "Me and yo daddy use to play basketball at the rec in the projects." If that doesn't work, then I might mention my grandmother or great grandmother's name.

Scenarios such as random run-ins at Walmart take place every day all around the world. The slight interrogation to learn more about one's family background is probably the oldest brand evaluation on the face of the Earth. Whether we want to or not, we carry the brands of our foreparents and the brands of those who were associated with them.

Throughout our formative years and into young adulthood, our given name serves as the foundation for our personal brands. The habits and character traits we develop then add to what we are already known by. Knowing this, I reflect on my own experiences.

When I entered this world, I was born with the brands created by Waymer & Julia Reed, Carolyn & Walter Reynolds, Margret & Alison Lee, Tom & Sally Boykin, Mattie Woods & Alphonso Sanford, and Machelle & Julyan Lee. I inherited the good and the bad that came with their brands and nothing can change that. The things that my foreparents, uncles, aunts and/or cousins did will forever be part of their brands and because of blood ties, mine. It is not within my power to erase the marks these people left on the world. What I can do, however, is rebrand with my life.

The projects, trailer parks, or the backwoods of Alabama do not define who we are or who we will become. The character traits that we unknowingly display, the way we approach situations, the people that we associate with, what we post on social media and even how we dress all make up who we really are. These things are our brands and dictate the future of our families.

I've realized that I am my ancestors' wildest dreams and, at the same time, the master of my own fate. I have the unique power to mold my future, and so do you. From the way you interact with your spouse, kids, supervisor or the man running the corner store, your brand is on display and it leaves more of an impression on others than you know.

I encourage you to evaluate everything that makes you,

you. Start changing the things about your brand that are within your power and stop focusing on the things that aren't. Break generational curses and replace them with generational wealth. Be clear, I'm not talking about just money here. I'm talking about a good name.

Create the perception that you want others to have by living the reality you've worked so hard to create. Ensure that what's said about you when you're not in the room reflects your last name and the things you've contributed to that name. Yes, my family name and your family name are brands of their own; however, we are far more than just that and the legacy continues with us.

Challenge:

Your last name is your first brand. Take what was given to you and make of it what you want. Be an active participant in the legacy you leave.

25 Trust Your Gift

To my chosen auntie - Cheryl Pepsii Riley

If open mic nights are the classrooms for musical artists, then New York City is the best school system I know. In my opinion these places serve as a breeding ground for emerging singers and musicians. It's a place where lessons are learned, growth takes place and creativity flows.

One in particular that has shaped my life is Black Velvet Mondays hosted by the legendary Cheryl Pepsii Riley. For over 15 years now, Cheryl and her band Hot Chocolate along with Team Horn Section have provided a safe place where singers and musicians continue to do what they've always done – surrender to the music.

Like so many others, Cheryl has become family to me and just like a blood relative, Auntie Cheryl not only keeps me in line, she also supports and pours into my professional and personal life. Early on she taught me one key thing, which just so happens to be the mantra for her open mic night. She would always say, "Trust Your Gift."

For years I heard her say this every Monday night and after a while the meaning started to evolve. The different meanings came when emphasizing each word in the phrase.

TRUST Your Gift

As a verb, the word trust means to believe in the reliability, truth, ability, or strength of someone or something. The word trust as a noun speaks to the firm belief in the reliability, truth, ability, or strength of someone or something. In order to be a noun the word trust must first be a verb. Meaning action. Meaning work. Meaning you can't have trust without first trusting.

Since I can't speak for you, I'll just talk about me. Early on in my career, I found it hard to trust what was inside of me. I just wanted a sign confirming that what I had to offer was valuable to others.

What I had to realize was that my trust was never meant to lie in the ability of others to recognize my gift, but in the gift itself. I had to know that the reason I am given opportunities to use my gift is because what I have to offer is needed. Once I understood this, I started to trust my gift even more.

Trust **YOUR** Gift

I don't care if you are on the stage, working backstage, in front of the stage, or if you built the stage; Trust YOUR Gift. The "your" is special because it assigns ownership and responsibility as well as speaks to just how unique and special your gift is to you.

Auntie Cheryl says that my gift is not supposed to sound or look like anyone else's gift, and I couldn't agree more. My gift is unique to me just like yours is unique to you. However, we both must trust our own. The good book says that YOUR gift will make room for YOU. Not your neighbor's, not your best friend's, not even ya momma's; YOUR gift!

Trust Your **GIFT**

Emphasizing the word "GIFT" speaks to what you have to offer. We often lose faith in our gifts when we see how many other people offer the same thing. I once heard that in the bread aisle of a grocery store, you'll see about a dozen different brands of bread. Bread in different package sizes, shapes and with different intended uses. However, it's all still bread.

Gifts are the same way. There may be a thousand other folks out there doing the same thing that you do; but, can't no one do what you do how you do it. It's what sets you a part. Just keep telling yourself the recipe may be the same however, you are the secret ingredient.

Whenever it feels like you've come to a plateau in your life, go back to the classroom and relearn how to Trust Your Gift. As Auntie Cheryl says, "We're just all learning to do what we've already learned how to do."

wisDOM:

Remember that your gift has value so trust what you have to offer and do it how you do it.

26 Only You Can Prevent Forest Fires

In 1944, The United States Department of Agriculture's Forest Service launched a campaign with a bear and a quote to raise awareness and action for wildlife preservation. By 1947 that quote was updated to "Only YOU Can Prevent Forest Fires." Although I first heard the slogan in the early '90s, it wasn't until my late twenties that I realized just how on point it was. Oblige me if you will…

Think of the world as a forest. Now consider yourself a tree in that forest. Look at you, growing, thriving, existing in all of your glory and in the space that is your own. Regardless of whether you are an evergreen, apple or palm tree, you grew from the same earth as every other tree; yet, you still managed to keep your uniqueness. No one else does being you like you do. Yeah, some may come close; however, there will never be another tree exactly like you.

Now as a tree, what you have to realize is that your existence is not just for you nor are you here just to be here. Oh no. You and everything about you exists for a purpose.

Your roots, as deep as they run, allow you to stand tall while holding the ground around you in place so that others can walk about and gaze at your wonder. Your trunk, full and sturdy, serves as shelter for animals and other creatures. Your leaves and the fruit you bear provide food for all kinds of animals to eat so that they can grow healthy and strong. Your limbs as far out and up as they reach are able to keep creatures below from overheating in the sun and protect them from the downpour of rain during a storm. You, just being who you were created to be, produce air for all to breathe. In so many ways you are a source of life. Do you hear me? Yes, You Give LIFE!

Baby girl, you are strong. You bend in the wind but never break. You grow season after season my brother and become renewed with every revolution around the sun. You are great and even in all of your greatness, you are not exempt from threats. Threats that come to keep you from being your best self and living out your purpose.

What are threats? A threat, if you will, is equivalent smoke. It's a preview of a coming attraction; a sign that something is not right. It is oftentimes ignored even though it can cloud the line of sight. So what are some threats to watch out for? Like to hear them? Here they go.

If you notice that a particular person's presence constantly makes you feel some type of way, that's smoke. When you realize that texting a certain person repeatedly throws your day off track, that's smoke. When you find that you can't focus on your focus because you have let other people's problems consume your thoughts, that's smoke.

The signs are all there. You just have to know your triggers and pay attention to the smoke signals. You control what gets you angry. You control who gets on your nerves. You control what ruins your day. Learn your triggers and learn who triggers you. These things are nothing but early signs of a fire brewing that could keep you from living out your purpose.

You, me, us. We're not exempt from threats. We each must know the value of our purpose and learn how to identify things that come to rob us of sharing it with the world. Because to be honest, only you can prevent your forest fires.

wisDOM:

Identify your triggers, know the value of what you bring to the table and protect it at all costs.

27 If You See Something, Say Something

"If you see a suspicious package or activity on the platform or train, do not keep it to yourself. Tell a Police Officer or an MTA employee. Remain alert and have a safe day. Remember, if you see something; say something."

If you've ever taken the New York City subway system, then you've probably heard this message before. The Metropolitan Transportation Authority uses this announcement to encourage riders to play an active role in their safety and wellbeing. Well, the same can be asked of all of us in our daily walk.

Life is accompanied with feelings; and more often than not, these feelings come at the hands of people and situations. These feelings do not equate weakness; in fact, they are what makes us human. It is important to feel every emotion that comes from life's happenings and it is equally important to express these feelings to those who caused them.

Letting someone know that something isn't right is imperative to their growth and your sanity!

Too many times we hold on to toxic relationships and remain in hurtful situations all in the name of love and loyalty or out of fear of what will happen next. This is what I call staying on a train knowing good and well it's headed in the wrong direction.

Now I'm guilty of it myself. I have been a willing participant in the undermining of my own character while damaging my inner being. I've knowingly, and unknowingly, allowed people to devalue my worth simply because of the title they held in my life. How? I'm glad you asked.

I never said those three words: "You hurt me." I never told them that what they said or did negatively impacted my self-confidence. Instead, I made allowances for their actions, shut up and just took it in silence. All along I was valid in my feelings. My feelings were real and I had the right to say something, regardless of whether they did it intentionally or unintentionally.

Some therapists say that the first step is acknowledgement. In other words, call that shit out! Hell, with knowledge comes responsibility and when you know better you should do better.

Now after you've said it plain and you realize that things still haven't changed, that's when you have to act accordingly. Be warned, this may look like removing yourself from the situation or distancing yourself from a particular person. And that's okay! It's alright to do what's best for you.

Look, you can't control anyone's actions except your own. As the conductor of your sanity, you determine what gets you upset and what doesn't. You have the authority to abort any relationship, situation and/or space that robs you of your peace.

In the beginning of my thirties, I realized that, contrary to popular belief, life is short. I'm only on this Earthly train for a little while and I'd be a damn fool if I let someone or something keep me from enjoying the ride. So nowadays if I see something, I'm saying something.

Challenge:

You have the right to be happy. If someone or something stands in the way of your happiness, speak up! You are valid in your feeling; so say something.

28 We Got Food at the House

I can't speak for you or how you were raised; I just know that Chell and Granny cooked. And cooked multiple times during the week at that. I'm talking baked, boiled or fried chicken, cornbread, collard greens, pot roast, meatloaf, spinach, string beans, country fried steak with mashed potatoes and gravy. We ate good y'all (lol) - we ate good!

Now I've got to be honest, every night wasn't Sunday dinner. Sometimes it was lasagna and a salad, a turkey sandwich and chips or just hot dogs – boiled, baked or fried with sauerkraut. Regardless, eating out was a privilege and oftentimes reserved for special occasions. But knowing this never stopped me from asking.

On a random Thursday after baseball practice or while out running errands on Saturday I would try my luck, just like thousands of kids around the country, and ask could we stop and get something to eat at a fast food joint. Probably one of the most commonly used responses to this request was, "You got some McDonald's money?"

You know you've heard it before. Even if McDonald's wasn't your restaurant of choice, then Burger King, Taco Bell or Sonic was substituted in its place. Growing up, I thought this question was insulting. Number one, it's rhetorical. Chell knew damn well I ain't have no McDonald's money! She was just being smart. And number two, when it's followed by, "We got food at the house", now that's just plain ole' punishment (lol)!

It wasn't until I got older that I realized the question "Do you have McDonald's money?" wasn't to insult my intelligence. Instead it was posed to make me differentiate between my wants and my needs. You see what I **wanted** was McDonald's, what I **needed** was nourishment.

I don't know about you, but in my adult life I've overdraft on a happy meal. Yuuup! A happy meal y'all! That five dollar want cost me $30 on the backend. And you would have thought that I would have learned my lesson the first time. Nope! This happened to me twice and on both occasions I had food at the house. It might have been leftovers, nonetheless it was food.

And since we're on the subject of leftovers, I've never minded them personally – even though Chell might argue otherwise (lol). Crazy thing is, as an adult, I am a champion for leftovers. The only difference is now I call it meal prep (humph). You laughing, but I don't care how we try to dress it up. If it's not consumed on the same day that it's cooked, it's leftovers (lol). Any who, I digress.

Sometimes, our wants and needs are not as simple as food and oftentimes they require conversations with ourselves. Here's a few talks I've had with myself:

Me: I need a vacation. Let's go to Paris.

Inner Me: *Dom, do you have Paris money?*

Or

Me: I need a new phone. Ooh, let's get the new iPhone

Inner Me: *Dom, do you have new iPhone money?*

Stop laughing! I know I'm not the only one.

Too many times, we as adults go to satisfy a need and end up doing the most. Spending too much money only to realize that our intentions of supplying our needs turned into us living outside of our means in order to satisfy our wants.

Today, I'm grateful that I didn't always get what I wanted. It taught me to be appreciative of what I already had. Too many of us adults weren't told as a child, "we got food at the house" and it shows. Do I now have McDonald's money? Yes, most days. However, I'd rather eat what's at the house now so that I can eat French fries in France later.

Challenge:

Learn the difference between your wants and needs. Curve your urges to splurge and practice being grateful for what you have.

29 The Cup and the Saucer

I'm not a big coffee drinker; I'm more of a tea guy (lol). In today's society, many of us drink coffee and/or tea on the go in a cup with a lid. However, if we ever order tea at a restaurant, it's typically served in a cup and saucer.

Psalm 23:5 KJV says, *"Thou preparest a table before me in the presence of mine enemies: thou anointest my head with oil; my cup runneth over."*

Indulge me for a second if you will. Envision that I'm a cup and God is constantly pouring things into my life. If this is the case, at some point I should start to overflow. I once heard a pastor say, "What's in the cup is for you. What's in the saucer is for someone else."

You read that right! The blessings that are being poured into my life are not only for me. The opportunities that I am being given are not only for me. The job that I have is not only for me. The level of success that I have is not only for me. These things also are for those around me.

Let me let you in on a little secret. Because people are connected to me, they get what I get. Because they are seated at my table, I know that these people around me are the recipients of my overflow blessings. And let me add that sometimes those people are my enemies.

Matthew 5:44 KJV backs the scripture in Psalms and says, *"But I say unto you, Love your enemies, bless them that curse you, do good to them that hate you, and pray for them which despitefully use you, and persecute you…"*

Yea, that's in your Bible too unless you tore it out.

So regardless of who it is, when I'm blessed; those around

me are blessed. When I eat, everyone at the table eats. God did not overload me with blessings just so I can keep them to myself. And who am I to hoard the overflow anyway? For years we've told ourselves the lie that any overflow we receive is for a rainy day. When in actuality, the extra was given so that we could make it rain on others.

Holding on to what we should be sharing in fear of not having enough speaks to our subconscious beliefs that God is incapable or unwilling to overflow us again. And if we're being honest; most times it is not that God will not do it again, it's that we are not ready for Him to do it again.

Thinking back to the cup and saucer, if you noticed, every saucer has a ring or a sunken place in the middle of it. This ring or sunken area is not there by mistake. No, it's actually intentional because it tells the one pouring if the cup is in the right position. If tilted and not in its proper position, the cup cannot hold its full capacity and the saucer ends up catching more overflow than intended. Help me Holy Ghost!

At times, others can receive more overflow than intended because we were not in the proper position. When we get in the right position, when we are obedient, when we remain humble, and when we maintain an attitude of gratitude, we will become full and what's intended for us will not spill over to our neighbors.

Listen, I'm not here to tell you how to live your life. I just want you to have life more abundantly. We should all be more intentional about getting in our proper places and sharing our overflow. We should get and remain in a state where God can use us to bless someone else. In doing so, I promise that we will all be fulfilled.

wisDOM:

What's for you is for you and everything else is for others. First get into position and then expect an overflow.

30 If You Can "Huh" Me, You Can Hear Me

Let me tell you something. If you grew up with a black momma or grand-momma, I'm pretty sure you've had a conversation that went something like this:

Chell: (calling from the other room) "Dominique, come here!"

Me: (hollering back) "Huh?"

Chell: (calling again from the other room – this time with a little more…. color) "Dominique, come here!!!"

Me: "Huh!?!"

Chell: (bussing through my bedroom door)

Me: (scared out my mind)

Chell: (now looking me dead in my face) "Dominique! I know you hear me calling you!!!"

Me: "I said, huh."

Chell: "If you can 'huh' me you can hear me!"

Now be honest, you know you read that in your momma's voice (lol)!

I do quite a bit of public speaking. Personally, I believe we are all created – or if you're spiritual: called – to do something. Me? I'm a communicator. Whether behind a podium, in a classroom, through this book or via a marketing campaign for a client's new song; all I do is communicate. However, I haven't always been comfortable doing so.

Awhile back, I identified communicators who I was

naturally drawn to. Some GOATS and some rising stars such as Oprah Winfrey, DeVon Franklin, Tiffany Haddish, Richard Pryor, Phylicia Rashad, Kenneth "Babyface" Edmonds, Whitney Houston, Dr. Martin Luther King Jr. and my Forever First Family – Barack and Michelle Obama all made the list. I studied their styles, rhythms and word choices. I dissected their posture and presentation and quickly discovered that I lacked a few things that I thought made them great.

Despite getting discouraged and starting to think that maybe I wasn't cut out to be a communicator, people still asked me to speak. So you know what I did? I kept talking. Slowly I became less worried about my inabilities and more confident in my abilities. With that confidence came the realization that what I had to offer wasn't for everyone. Not everyone was going to hear what I had to say.

In John 10:27 KJV, God says, *"My sheep hear my voice and I know them and they follow me..."* Now I'm not God, nor do I want to be. However, when I understood as a communicator that not everyone is assigned to me, I no longer got upset when my words didn't move people. Those who are assigned to me will hear my voice, they will "huh" me, and receive what I have to say because it's tuned to a frequency that they can hear and understand.

You see, I don't always use correct grammar. I'm more fluent in shade than I am in English. I talk in parables, with my hands and sometimes in circles. My facial expressions often say more than my words and let's keep it all the way a buck: I'm country as hell and I cuss (lol). I am aware that everyone is not going to hear or receive a message through the censored beeps. However, those who can hear me, will. And those are my people.

My modes of communication are not for everyone and the same goes for you. Create your way, speak in your voice, and write in your style because your delivery is unique to you. Can't nobody do what you do the way you do it. God has tuned your tone, your word choice and your voice frequency to the ears of a set number of people.

Never mind the majority that's not assigned to you. Your role is to talk it how you talk it. Just speak up for the people in the back who are hard of hearing and take comfort in knowing that if they can "huh" you, they can hear you.

wisDOM:

Can't nobody put words in your mouth when you're telling your own story. Talk it how YOU talk it.

31 Call a Spade a Spade

I have a confession. I am a Black man. A graduate of a Historically Black University, an affiliate of several black circles and organizations and yet, I do not know how to play spades. I've been taught countless of times over the years and I just can't seem to get it. I've come to terms with this. I will forever be the bartender; keeping the drinks flowing for those seated at the table. But that's not what this segment is about so stop judging me.

I have this theory. I believe that each of us has one ongoing trauma that takes us years to acknowledge and just as long to overcome. It's like a thorn in our sides that start out as a small bump and over the years grows into much more. It shows up in different forms and in different areas of our lives. It's something that we unconsciously battle with daily.

This flaw, if you will, oftentimes has deep roots and we accept and/or downplay it with the phrase, "Oh that's just who I am." When in actuality it's not.

For years I knew I had a thorn, but it never hurt me enough to fix it. It would show up sporadically, hurt for a while then go back into hiding and I would forget all about it. To be honest, I never really called it by name until after years of neglect I started to recognize the negative effects of it going untreated.

At age 29, I really started to notice that I wasn't happy. A year later, I circled back and realized that nothing had changed. That's because time does not heal all wounds and nothing changes unless I change.

For a week straight this thing hit me in the face every day. No more summer visitations, it was here to stay. At work, in conversation with friends, even while at a concert.

It seemed like wherever I went, it met me there. Hell, by the time I made it to the following Sunday, I damn near expected it. And sure enough it showed up. At this point I could not keep avoiding it any longer. After seven days of riding my back, I finally called a spade a spade.

"Comparison." I finally said it. I battled with comparison and had done so since grade school.

You see in elementary school I made what now seems like silly non-threating comparisons to my friends. My broken home to their full house. My darker skin tone to their brighter completion. My nappy roots to their "good" grade of hair. My height to their height. Small seeds right?

By the time I was leaving high school and heading into college those seeds grew into full blown low self-esteem. I began to see myself as less than my counterparts. I started to not like the sound of my own voice and how I spoke. Because I was always in the friend zone, I also thought that I was the least attractive in my crew.

Now this could have gone several ways. For some, it could have turned into envy, jealousy and caused hatred and anger to form like a bitter taste in the mouth. However, it caused me to over compensate in areas that weren't subjective to others' opinions.

If you knew me back then, you might claim that I'm lying because I appeared to be confident and always leading in some capacity. But what folks don't know is that I would use those depressing feelings as motivation to excel in the things that were factual and could not be debated, argued or taken away from me.

After graduating college this battle with comparison started to take the form of me looking and liking folks pictures on Instagram and wanting to be them. Yeah, I grew out my hair, started buying new clothes and I still could not compete with their style or swag.

When I finally called comparison by name, I started to see myself whole. As beautifully flawed as I am, I began to accept and promote my uniqueness. I started to realize that I, Dominique J. Lee, was intentionally created to be uniquely me and that there was room for me to show up in the world as me.

God began to tell me, and I began to believe, that I was created and set aside for such a time as this. I am not too short. My voice is not too high. My nose is not too wide. My hairline – as sketchy as it is – and the amount of melanin in my skin is enough.

Nowadays comparison doesn't visit me as often and it's all because I decided to treat what was hurting me. If I'd continued to let comparison cripple me, I would have never written this book. Those assigned to my voice would never hear what I was created to say. And you? You would never know my name nor my story.

Now, I want the same for you. Whatever it is that you are battling, be it pride, envy, gluttony, lust, anger, greed or sloth, call a spade a spade and start treating those traumas now. Because someone in this world needs you to be your best self. Ask me how I know!

Challenge:

You are enough. Flawed but enough. Broken but enough. Hurt but enough. Identify the areas that are keeping you from believing that and grow past it.

The Ride Home

Red Cup Philosophy Acknowledgements

Experiencing a red cup party feels like a high that no one wants to come down from. On the ride home and even during the days following, the memories replay over and over again in our minds. The laughs, the conversations, the epiphanies and all of the feels randomly bring a smile to our faces. I had a red cup experience writing this book and I hope you got the same reading it.

But just like with any party, the memories mean nothing without the people who were there with you shooting in the gym. First off, can I just thank God for Jesus? It's a rhetorical question because I'm going to do it anyhow (lol). Without the man above, none of this would be possible. So Thank You God for giving this opportunity to me. And to everyone mentioned in this book, I thank God for you too. I would not have had an encounter that brought about a lesson if you weren't present in my life. Thank You.

To my immediate family - Mom, Dad, Janice, Jarrod and Cameron - thanks for being a loving and supportive foundation. I know I can be the life of the party (lol), but you all have always been the first to arrive. Thank You! To my extended family, whether you or yo' momma 'nem last name is Lee, Stephens, Samford, Boykins, Reed, Reynolds, or Woods - Thank You! I may not get the chance to physically see or talk to y'all regularly; however, every time I do, I never leave empty.

Ashley Oliver… What can I say about you? Plenty (lol)! The days when writer's block gripped me, the nights when fear crippled me and the mornings when clarity found me, you were there and you handled my ego and attitude with grace and strength. This writing process would have been hell without you. Thank You. To my best friends, from grade school to college, Takova Wallace-Gay, Kelli Owens and Soniel Duncan, you ladies have given me the room to grow and live without judgement. Thank You. To my boys - Derrick M. Fleming Jr., Jarvis Hampton, Jerome' Holston, James Johnson and Tymon Graham; you keep me humble yet aware of my worth. Each of you add value to my life and hold a special place in my heart. Thank You.

Tonya Forde – Thank You. You get me and you genuinely believe in me. I am so happy our paths crossed. Now I can't forget my little brothers Dominique Foster and Colby Hollman. You two have allowed me to mentor you and in return you have mentored me. You have taught me so much about life and myself. I am beyond proud of the men you two are; men of action and character. I am humbled to know each of you. Thank You!

To my chosen families, who I dare not attempt to list by name because I know I'll miss someone (lol), Thank You.

Many of you were present during my childhood and adult red cup parties. You've poured into my life and the best decision I've made to date has been to choose you as my sisters, brothers, mothers, fathers, grams, aunties, uncles, nieces, nephews and dare I say it, children (lol). I'm so grateful for each of you. (looks to the left) "Hey Framily!!!" You know who you are. Y'all have adopted this southern soul and allowed me to simply be. The jokes, the shade, the support is always on time and needed. Thank You for continuing to hold me down while lifting me up. I promise to never stop asking the hard hitting questions. I love y'all.

A special Thank You to Antonio Johnson – who helped me develop the title of this book, Robert Mercer Jr. of Robert Mercer Jr Photography, Parrish Dove of P.Dove Creates, Kioshana Burrell of 2911 publishing, LaTasha M. McPherson and everyone who participated in the pre-reads for this book. You've lent your time, gifts and talents in the creation of this work. I would not have a book without you.

Last but not least... my brothers, my brothers. To the brothers of Alpha Kappa Psi, Professional Business Fraternity, Incorporated, with a special shout out to the Kappa Phi Chapter; thanks and much luv mane. And to the ice cold brothers of Alpha Phi Alpha Fraternity, Incorporated, with special gratitude to the Kappa Xi Lambda Chapter also known as The Wall Street Alphas; I am humbled by your support and encouragement.

Whelp... that's it. The party's over. Thank You for

coming and Thank You for opening your minds and making room in your hearts for me. I hope you had a good time reading because the words on these pages were written with you in mind. I intentionally shared my experiences because that's the only way the lessons would reflect the parallels in your own lives. I pray that you start acknowledging the unexpected yet significant moments that shape who you are.

Moments that cause you to think more deeply, see yourself more clearly and live more abundantly. I'm sure by now you've already realized a few of your own red cup philosophy moments because life is nothing but a big red cup party (lol). But until the next time you hear the music blasting and the Bar-B-Que smoke rising from the back porch keep living, keep learning and know that I love you family. Cheers!